HOW TO SOLVE A PROBLEM

The Rise (and Falls) of a Rock-Climbing Champion

ASHIMA SHIRAISHI

illustrations by Yao Xiao

MAKE ME A WORLD

New York

To my aunt Kay, thanks for teaching me to believe
—A.S.

For my grandmothers,
who showed me that creativity and perseverance
can make all the difference
—Y.X.

MAKE ME A WORLD is an imprint dedicated to exploring the vast possibilities of contemporary childhood. We strive to imagine a universe in which no young person is invisible, in which no kid's story is erased, in which no glass ceiling presses down on the dreams of a child. Then we publish books for that world, where kids ask hard questions and we struggle with them together, where dreams stretch from eons ago into the future and we do our best to provide road maps to where these young folks want to be. We make books where the children of today can see themselves and each other. When presented with fences, with borders, with limits, with all the kinds of chains that hobble imaginations and hearts, we proudly say—no.

Library of Congress Cataloging-in-Publication Data is available upon request.
ISBN 978-1-5247-7327-4 (trade) — ISBN 978-1-5247-7328-1 (lib. bdg.) — ISBN 978-1-5247-7329-8 (ebook)

The illustrations in this book were created digitally.
Book design by Nicole de las Heras
Printed in the United States of America
April 2020
10 9 8 7 6 5 4 3
First Edition

Dear Reader,

The first time I met Ashima Shiraishi, we talked about hip-hop, books, and dessert. She is a teenager, and curious about all the things that teenagers are curious about. For a moment, one could almost forget that she is one of the best in the world at what she does. At the end of our meeting, I ask what she's doing next. She says she will go practice, by which she means she will face a wall for four hours. She will climb it again and again. She will work on holds and techniques. She will make mistakes. And make them again. Until she learns how to do it better.

Being the best in the world is not something we are born into. Ashima's parents aren't climbers; they are artists, New Yorkers. Her mom loves to sew, and still makes the pants Ashima climbs in. Her father was a dancer. The kind of guy who takes his young daughter to Central Park, and lets her climb the rocks because it's fun, not knowing there is a champion inside her. Being the best in the world is made of countless hours in the gym. It's made of mistakes and falls. It's the discipline and care and the time it takes to go back to that wall and try again. The ability to try again after failing—that is what it takes to be great. That might be Ashima's greatest superpower.

I imagine every child might like to be the best in the world at something. And I know of no better guide than this teenager who likes hip-hop, books, and dessert. Who, after school, will go to a wall in Queens or Brooklyn, and keep working on that wall—that "problem," as a climber would say—until she has solved it.

Christopher Myers

MAKE ME A WORLD

I am Ashima.
What I do is climb.
What I do is solve problems,
which is to say, I make them mine.

We climbers call our boulders problems.

We also call our problems problems—
and to solve them both is sort of the same.

Once I had a problem and it stretched into the sky.
It was tremendously endless.

It was bigger than thinking.

It was as huge as the air or the night or the planet.

It was a problem bigger than any

I had ever seen,

and I have seen plenty.

There were twists and turns.
There were places that looked as slick as glass.

One part was arched like a question mark,
another part stuck out like my father's elbow
in a photo I have seen of him dancing,
and another was shaped like the bolts of fabric
stacked in my mother's sewing room.

There were many parts,
and none of them looked easy.

I sighed, and clapped my hands full of chalk (which is what I do before I solve a problem).

I held this problem in my head,
I mapped out every step—
each place I would put my hand—
and then I began to climb.

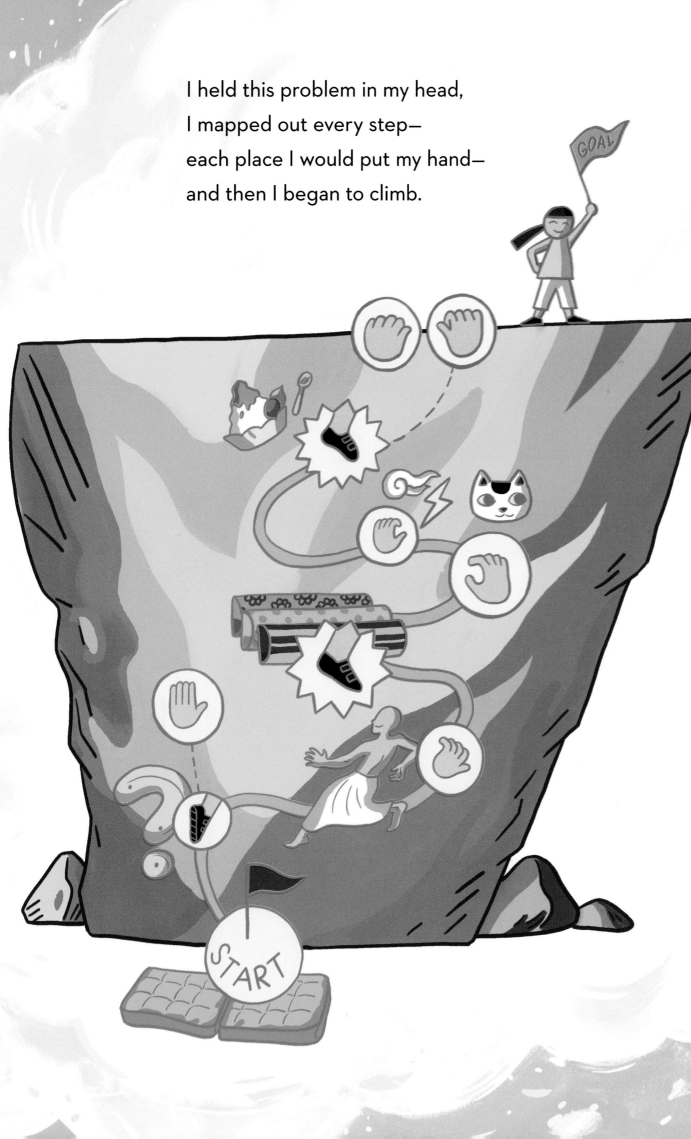

Dug my toe into the dot of
the question mark,

jammed my fingertips into the bend
of my father's dancing elbow,

kicked my leg over my
mother's fabrics.

I was climbing on nothing but air.

And then, for a moment, the world slipped out from under me.

The ground beneath me rushed up
and pressed into my back,
like the hand of a giant, named gravity.

So I dusted myself off.
Dad asked how I was feeling.
He passed me a peanut butter and jelly sandwich,
and for a while we just sat there.

Then, when I was ready,
I looked at the problem again,
with the new information
the fall had given me.

Each fall is a message, a hint, an idea.

A new way to move from over there to over here.

And so I started.
And so I fell.
And so I climbed again,
listening to what the fall had told me—

the problem that was endless,
which I broke into little pieces;
the problem that gave me hints
with each fall—

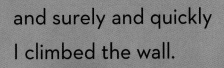

and surely and quickly
I climbed the wall.

I dug my fingers there and here
and stretched my arms like ropes.

I threw my body through the air
and caught myself in all the ways I'd imagined,
a bright path of thinking.

And there, at the top of the problem,
I looked down
at the bolts of fabric,
the dot of the question mark,
the bend of the elbow,

and I waved hello at the memory of how hard the problem was.

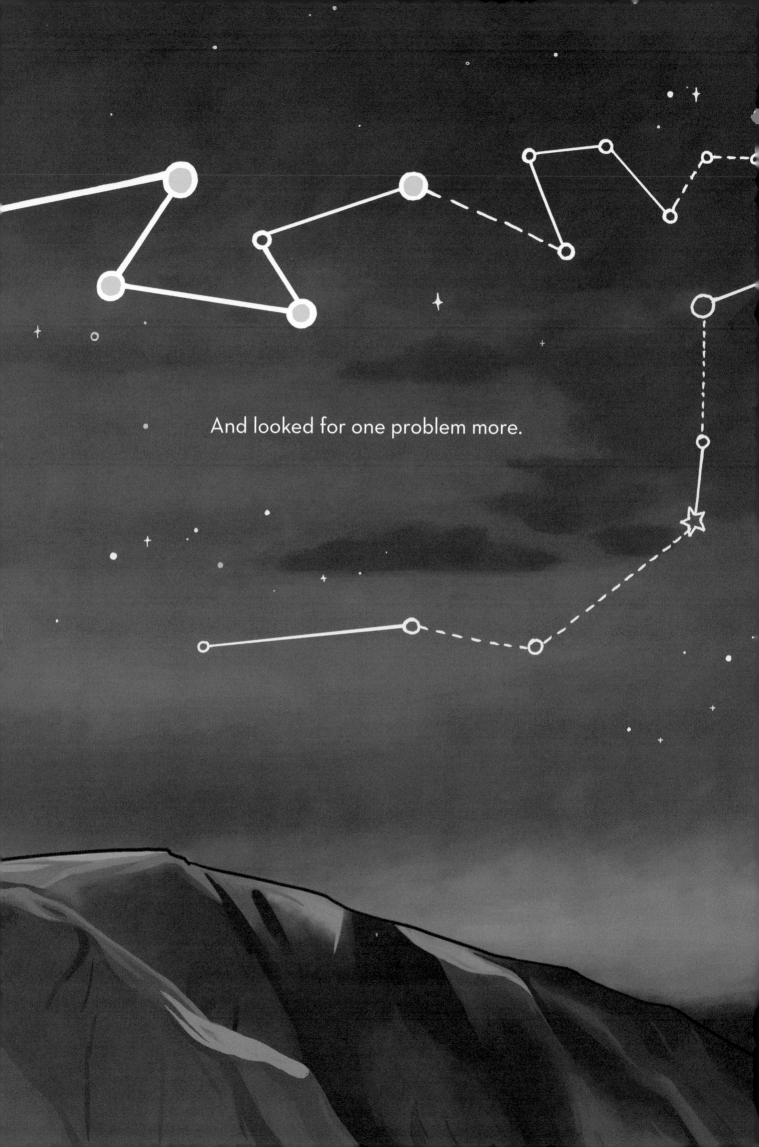

And looked for one problem more.

Age 9

Ashima climbs
her first
V11 and V12 problems,
including *Rogered in
the Shower* and
Chablanke in
Hueco Tanks.

Age 8

Ashima solves
the problem
Power of Silence in
Hueco Tanks, Texas.
This boulder is rated
V10 for difficulty—
a grade only
expert climbers
can achieve.

Age 7

Ashima enters
her first climbing
competition.

Age 6

Ashima begins
climbing at
Rat Rock
in Central Park,
New York City.

April 3, 2001

Ashima Shiraishi
is born to Tsuya and
Hisatoshi Shiraishi.

Data is not available
for when Ashima
figures out how to
climb out of her crib.

ASHIMA'S ASCENT

Age 10

Ashima becomes the youngest person ever to climb a V13 problem: *Crown of Aragorn* in Hueco Tanks. Only elite climbers and professionals can climb at this grade.

Age 13

Ashima climbs *Golden Shadow* in Rocklands, South Africa (pictured in this book!), her first V14.

Age 14

Ashima becomes the first woman in the world to climb a V15 boulder problem: *Horizon* in Mount Hiei, Japan. She is the second person ever to solve this problem.

Age 15

Ashima sweeps the IFSC Youth World Championships for her third year running and also places first in SCS Nationals.

What Comes Next?

The sky's the limit!